I0163014

Australian Animals

By JOwen

Library For All Ltd.

Library For All is an Australian not for profit organisation with a mission to make knowledge accessible to all via an innovative digital library solution. Visit us at libraryforall.org

Australian Animals

First published 2022

Published by Library For All Ltd
Email: info@libraryforall.org
URL: libraryforall.org

This work is licensed under the Creative Commons Attribution-NonCommercial-NoDerivatives 4.0 International License. To view a copy of this license, visit http://creativecommons.org/licenses/by-nc-nd/4.0/.

Our Yarning logo design by Jason Lee, Bidjipidji Art

Original illustrations by Meg Turner

Australian Animals
JOwen
ISBN: 978-1-922795-69-4
SKU01403

Australian Animals

We respect and honour Aboriginal and Torres Strait Islander Elders past, present and future. We acknowledge the stories, traditions and living cultures of Aboriginal and Torres Strait Islander peoples on this land and commit to building a brighter future together.

Crocodile

Dingo

Echidna

Emu

Lizard

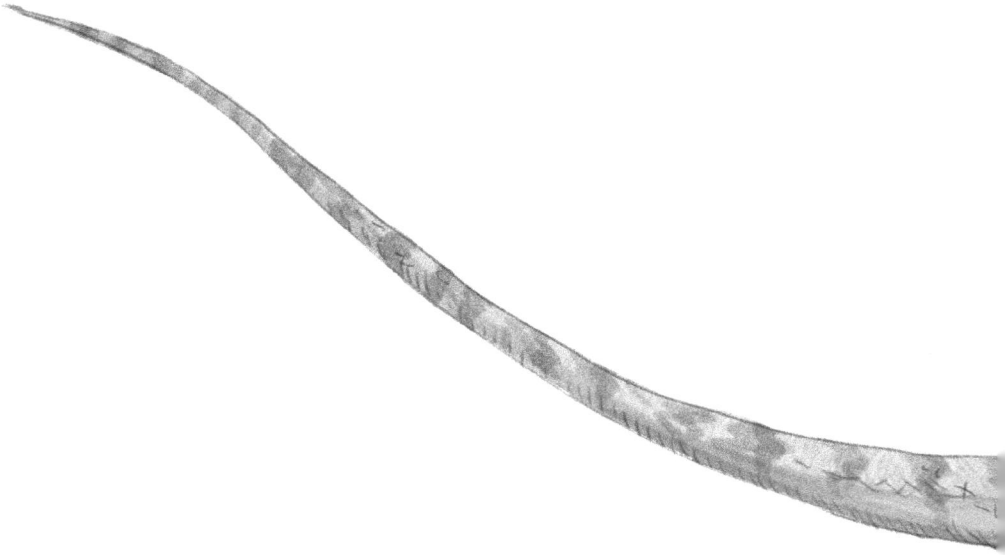

Kangaroo

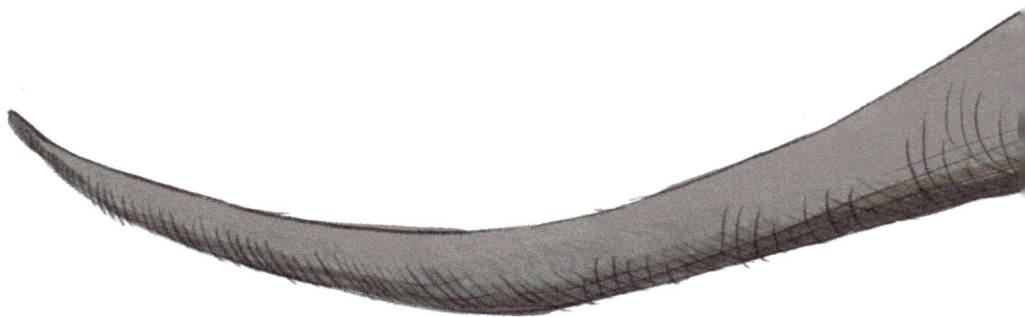

Koala

Wombat

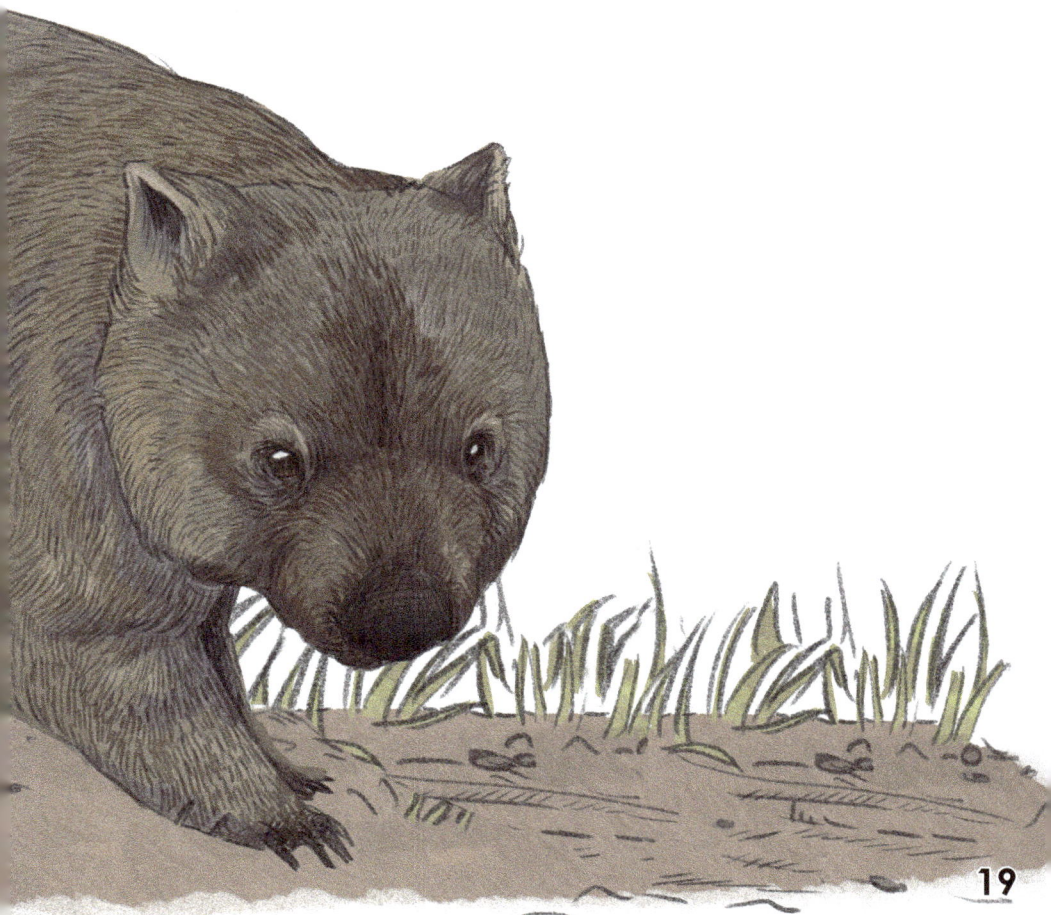

You can use these questions to talk about this book with your family, friends and teachers.

What did you learn from this book?

Describe this book in one word. Funny? Scary? Colourful? Interesting?

How did this book make you feel when you finished reading it?

What was your favourite part of this book?

download our reader app
getlibraryforall.org

About the author

JOwen is from the Nurrunga/Ngarrindjeri Nations of South Australia. She was born in Adelaide and now lives in Broome, Western Australia. She loves the laughs and fun of family gatherings. As a child her favourite book was *I Can Jump Puddles.*

Our Yarning

Want to discover more books from this collection? Our Yarning is a collection of books written by Aboriginal and Torres Strait Islander peoples across Australia.

We know that children learn better, and enjoy reading more, when they see themselves in the stories, characters and illustrations of the books they read.

To download the app, visit the Google Play Store on any Android device and search 'Our Yarning'.

libraryforall.org

www.ingramcontent.com/pod-product-compliance
Lightning Source LLC
Chambersburg PA
CBHW042346040426

42448CB00019B/3419